Everything I Needed To Know About Network Marketing I Learned From My Kids!

Keri McKee

Published by William Direct, Inc.
Las Vegas, Nevada
wmdirect@earthlink.net

ISBN: 0-9743028-0-5

This book is dedicated to my husband Mark, who has a true gift of passion and purpose that inspires others to reach for the stars. And to my children, Kailee, Eric, Tyler, Jenna, and Max, who fill everyday with love and excitement!

Contents

Introduction

Today I took my 5 year old Tyler to his friend's house down the street. He was on his bike as I walked down the driveway. It was a typical spring morning in Las Vegas, a comfortable 80 degrees, not a cloud in the sky. Tyler said," Isn't it a beautiful day, Mom?"

I had to admit it was a perfect morning. He then asked me, "Why when I go outside in the morning are all the birds squeaking?"

I told him they were singing their songs. He looked at me with a warm gaze and said, "I just love them!"

To be able to see the world through the eyes of a child. They appreciate the little things that adults either take for granted or overlook entirely in their rush to get through the day. To live in the moment. Children are experts at living in the here and now.

I am the mother of five, and appreciate the ways that children perceive and interact with their world. They are not burdened with the heavy baggage adults drag around everyday. They live for each moment, and expect to get what they want. They don't hesitate to communicate their feelings and you pretty much know where you stand with a child, like it or not!

When a child has a goal in mind, they set out with gusto to achieve it. When my children want something, they possess a persistence that is stronger than the most seasoned, successful network marketer you have ever met. In fact, their persistence is often mistaken for stubbornness and punished by a time out in their room. It's a fine line we walk as parents and I often wonder how to instill the positive while maintaining a functional household.

I wrote this book because, as I have spent my first 2 years in network marketing, I have drawn on the lessons I have learned from 16 years of raising children. Network marketing is a people business, and what better way to learn about people than to observe them from birth to adulthood.

There are many correlations between starting and building your own home-based business and starting and raising a family. My husband and I have become better parents from the personal growth we have experienced in becoming successful in our business. And we have had better results in our business because of the lessons we have learned from raising our children.

That is why we love network marketing. This industry allows us to live our values. We have the ability through financial and time freedom to put our family first. That may sound like a cliché and it may sound simplistic, but it is so powerful and it is simple.

In network marketing we get to help people help themselves. The more people we help, the more money we make. We set an example for our children by showing how to control your life, spend time with the people that are most important to you, and have a positive impact on the world. It is such a synergistic lifestyle. The better person you are, the better your business is, and the better your family is.

Whether you have children or not, you once were a child yourself, and will enjoy going back to childhood experiences and picking out the "ah- has" that you can apply to your business. If you are thinking of becoming a parent, you will realize that your network marketing business is providing you with valuable skills and personal growth that will add to your family relationships.

So, experience life through a child's eyes. Look for the laughter. Have fun. Expect the best. Enjoy the now. You will be amazed at how many people you will attract into your life and business. Don't be afraid to go for it. You will fall down a few times, but it is a miracle what a kiss and a band-aid can do for the ego!

I wish you much happiness and success in your life!

He not busy being born is busy dying.

Bob Dylan

Chapter One

Giving Birth - Starting Out

There is a very popular quote heard often in the network marketing industry: "It's much easier to give birth to a new distributor, than resurrect a dead one." I am certain that a man came up with that line because I have given birth to five children and I don't remember any of them being easy. In fact, they were all quite painful, but definitely rewarding experiences!

If we compare starting out in network marketing to a pregnancy, conception would be the day you enrolled with your company. The first trimester, you might experience some morning sickness. Your fears set in and you worry, "Am I ready for this child (your new home based business)? Do I know what I'm getting into?"

Your sponsor asks you to make a list, contact your family and friends. The thought of rejection may make you feel nauseous. But, if you have the support and systems of your company to plug into, it is like nibbling on soda crackers, and pretty soon your stomach settles.

Your second trimester brings on needed energy. The morning sickness is gone and you start to feel alive with a renewed purpose. You have been trained, use the systems and feel more and more comfortable talking to people. You hand out information about your business, and see some results. It's like experiencing your baby's first kicks. You are excited as you can visualize your business maturing.

Then comes the third trimester. You are tired. As your baby is getting bigger there is stress that comes with it. Now that you have your own "downline", you have to train and support them, while still keeping up your momentum. You will be disappointed with the performance of some, while trying to keep up with the performance of others.

You may still encounter rejection and have to focus on your dreams and goals to keep moving forward. At times it can be painful. My advice is to suck it up, give yourself a mental epidural, and keep pushing! With extreme focus and commitment, you will give birth to a fantastic business that will provide you with financial and personal freedom to enjoy for the rest of your life.

If you don't give birth to your business, your sponsor may resuscitate you once or twice, but will soon realize their time is better spent giving birth themselves.

To accomplish great things, we must dream as well as act.

Anatole France

Chapter Two

Dream Building

Network marketing offers everyone the opportunity to live the ultimate lifestyle of financial and time freedom. Your age, gender, race, religion, education, background, or past experience does not matter. If you have massive desire to improve your life and are committed to putting in some time each week, consistently, for 2-5 years, you can live your dream.

Dream building is the emotional connection needed to spark action for a prospect to join your business, and for you and your associates to keep moving forward. If you want to increase your sign- up rate, you need to increase your ability to get others to unlock, identify, and own their dreams.

When you show people the amazing benefits that network marketing provides, sometimes it seems too good to be true. I feel dream building is a process. You take people from where they are now, and step by step, build their dream. You need to take them to a place in their mind where they think like a child and anything becomes possible.

For instance, if you are talking to a single mom about the HUGE money she can make with your company, and she is worried about having the power shut off, chances are she won't be able to relate to the image you're painting. Her dream at the moment is to have a little more money coming into her life to relieve her of the financial pressure of everyday living.

Instead, talk to her about how it would FEEL to start making enough money in the next few months to not only help with the bills, but to start her children in sports or private music lessons. Have her picture the smiles on her children's faces when she tells them they can join a soccer team or learn to play the guitar. How will she feel to know she could provide her family with a few extras without the stress of finding a way to pay for them?

When she starts nodding as she stares off into space, you know you've awakened her dreams. Now take it a step further and tell her, if she sticks with it, 6 months from now, she could be paying off bills, planning family vacations, actually saving money for the kids college. Ask her if she can see it.

When she can, go another step and tell her there are many single moms in this business, that after a few years of consistent work are living a fantasy life, making huge walk- away incomes and spending unlimited time with their families. Many started in more dire straits than her, piled miles high in debt, with no formal education, but they had a *burning desire.*

When you build a bridge and take a person from their current reality to where their dreams are and show them that you will be traveling together on that bridge, they start to believe. Their imagination allows for the possibility that they can achieve their dreams.

It is so important to show them their life can change immediately as a result of this business. Make sure to impress on people that a few years of work in this industry can lead to a lifetime of money and the time freedom to enjoy it, but don't promise big money next week. Instead, choose a small but significant goal that can be realistically achieved, and would make a huge emotional difference in that person's world.

I know when I am trying to motivate my 3 and 5 year old to go along with me, if I can't show them an immediate benefit that they can experience within the next 30 seconds, I'm doomed. They don't want to hear about how much fun we are going to have at the park 3 hours from now. They want their desires met immediately.

We are a society that is programmed for instant gratification. Very few people maintain the focus, determination and commitment to reach their dreams.

So throw people a bone, give them a place to start. As they start seeing dream after dream come true, they develop trust in themselves, in you, and will go after their bigger dreams. That's when your business takes off, when you have lots of people chasing big dreams!

If you want to learn how much fun dream building can be, watch a child. They possess an infinite imagination and use it constantly as they play, learn and grow. Their world is full of possibilities, and if you try to tell them something isn't real or will not happen, observe the look of complete disbelief on their face.

Children have the precious gift of unshakable belief and that is what we need to combat the "Dream stealers" that we will inevitably run up against as we build our network marketing business.

Unlike children, most of us have years of "lack" or "scarcity" programming that tells us "Don't dream big."
" Be happy with what life dealt you."
" You don't deserve more."
" Big dreams are for a select few."

We start out life thinking we can have it all, but most end up in a rut, settling for less than we really want.

If you ask our eleven year old, Eric what he wants to be when he grows up he will say a comedian like Jim Carey AND a moto cross racer like Rickey Carmichael. He sees no reason to limit his choices.

14

He can be both. He knows there are obstacles and hard work ahead if he wants to live his dream, but the payoff far exceeds the cost in his mind. As he grows, his dreams may change, but I hope the conviction and commitment to reach them stays with him.

When you identify your dreams, you must start living them, even if it at first is only in your mind. Our son Tyler has loved Disney movies since he was two. You should see him get ready to watch one. We don't dare turn the VCR on until he has all his "stuff". He has props for every movie and he uses them to act out his part.

At one time his favorite movie was "Beauty and the Beast." He liked to play the part of Gaston. He had a cape, a belt, a plastic coat hanger (his bow), hot wheel tracks in different lengths (his swords), and a few other odds and ends that he would gather before the movie started. If anything were missing, he would search the house until he found it, because he would not enjoy the movie unless he was living it himself. He knew all the words and we have him on video watching his videos!

What about you? Do you have a movie script in your mind of what your "Dreams" are? Do you have a plan to live them? Have you started putting your props together and practicing your lines? Do you own your dreams? A child does not question the right to dream. Why do we?

Your dreams must be bigger than your fears to motivate you into action. They have to be real. You have to visualize them in your mind, be able to feel, taste, hear, see, and touch them. Be very detailed about how you want your life to be, what you would like to do and with whom you would like to do it with.

Take an afternoon and make a movie script of your "Dreams," creating your perfect life. Read it every day. Make a plan to start achieving it and living it now.

What can you do today that will bring you closer to your dreams? In 90 days what should you be doing? 6 months? 1 year? 5 years? Have a plan, and more importantly, start to act it out. There are little things that you can do today that are part of living your dreams.

Dream big! You deserve to. Like a child, you can see opportunities that are in your reach and you can grow from there. The best part is that the life you live while chasing your dreams is going to be a fantastic journey. You will smile more, laugh more, and touch more people.

You gain strength, courage and confidence by every experience in which you really stop to look fear in the face. You are able to say to yourself, "I have lived through this horror. I can take the next thing that comes along." You must do the thing you think you cannot do.

Eleanor Roosevelt

Chapter Three

Getting Out Of Your Comfort Zone

One of the hardest things to do in network marketing, and one of the keys to your success, is to step out of your comfort zone. It is what keeps most people stuck, because of the fear of the unknown. When we are in our comfort zone, we feel safe. It may not be where we dream about being, but we know what to do when we are there. We know what to expect and we don't have to confront our fears.

Whether it is approaching people about your business, speaking in front of people, daring to dream big, being a leader, traveling to an event, or working on yourself and addressing personal issues that may be holding you back, we all have areas that terrify us. It is much easier to stay where you are than to take a step forward.

It's like the story about the old dog on the front porch. A little boy asks his grandfather why the dog is moaning as it lays on the porch. The grandfather tells him it is because he is lying on a nail. The little boy asks why the dog doesn't just move. The grandfather tells him it doesn't hurt enough to move, just enough to moan about it!

Sometimes the pain isn't strong enough to get us out of our comfort zone and moving towards our dreams. It would mean change and we humans resist change.

Our son, Tyler, is definitely not one for change. He likes things to be routine. He puts his clothes on a certain way. He has to have his breakfast shake made the same way every morning. If his preschool teacher rearranges the room, it is unsettling to him. In the middle of this year, his teacher felt he was ready to move up a room. He flipped. He made his teacher promise that he could stay in her room until kindergarten. It was all he could think about. Before he went to bed at night he talked about it. Everyday he reminded me that he could stay in Mrs. Alanis's room. Because of his initial reaction, we all agreed that it would be fine to leave him in the same room.

But then we started feeling maybe that wasn't the best idea. Tyler was developmentally ready to move up. It was his fears that were holding him back. And we were reinforcing those fears by allowing him to stay in his comfort zone. What was that teaching him about life? That it is better to do nothing when

18

you are afraid. That change is scary and there must be a reason, because even Mommy and Daddy say it's better to stay where I am now.

So we bit the bullet and told the school we wanted him to move up to the next class. He was stressed out about the idea, to say the least. We kept reassuring him that he would love it, that he would learn fun things and that he would still get to see his old teacher. We told him that it was part of getting older. As you learn and grow, you try new things so you can have more fun.

The first day of his new class came and he was very nervous, and I have to admit I was wondering if we were pushing him emotionally. I took him to his class, he gave me an unsure look, held back the tears and one of his teachers took him by the hand. He was out of his comfort zone. I was out of mine too. I hate when my kids are upset. All day, I thought about Tyler at school.

When I picked Tyler up, he was playing in his new class. His teachers told me he was a little unsure at first, but after he settled in he did great. The next day was a little better and by the third day he was an old pro. He has been in his new class three months and is so proud of himself. He writes words on his own and has even learned to read.

I think about how we would have cheated him if we had taken the easy road and kept him in his old classroom. He wouldn't have experienced the self-satisfaction of personal growth. He will enter kindergarten with more confidence and skills. He has come out of his shell and amazed the teachers and staff with his bright personality. He is more willing to try new things because he knows it can be a positive experience. Last night he led the pre- K graduation ceremony and carried the US flag with a smile from ear to ear. I was so proud as we all said the pledge of allegiance.

I learned from this experience that just because someone is afraid to do something, it doesn't mean they can't do it. Trust in yourself and in others and take the chance. Stretch and get out of your box. The more you step out of your comfort zone, the easier it gets and the better you feel about yourself. Your dreams are waiting for you on the other side! You will experience new and amazing things; your comfort zone will expand and you will touch and inspire more people.

You can make more friends in two months by becoming interested in other people than you can in two years by trying to get other people interested in you.

Dale Carnegie

Chapter Four

Make Your List and Prospect

We have been told that we are not in business if we don't have a contact list of at least 100 names. It is our starting point, it creates our posture and it is the one thing that over 90 % of us put off doing. We come up with the lamest excuses of why we don't need it, or how we don't know that many people. We think of ten people, start contacting them (maybe) and then when we have made it through "our list" either quit by saying, "I gave it a try," or just procrastinate and say "I'll do it tomorrow."

We are in the people business, yet we are afraid of the small task of writing down one hundred names of people we know, let alone contacting them! If this is an overwhelming task for you, approach it in a different way with a different mindset.

Unless you are a hermit and never leave your home, an easy way to put a list together is to make it a point to start conversations with people wherever you go in your everyday activities. I'm not saying to start conversations about your network marketing business with everyone you meet. Over half of them you wouldn't want in your business anyway! Just have friendly conversations where your main purpose is to get to know the person.

Chances are if you make a connection, they will ask you about what you do and that is the perfect time to say, "Let me get your email, phone number or address and I'll get you information about my exciting business. I don't have the time to tell you about it now, but you could check out some information and if you're interested, we could go from there."

If someone has done a great job providing you with a service, then express how much you appreciated their help and ask for their business card. They will gladly hand you one in the hope of repeat business. Be sure and give them one of yours and let them know you will stay in touch. These are just a couple of ways to get names and start prospecting without the fear and stress of rejection hanging over your head, because your goal is to MAKE A FRIEND, not sell them on your business.

We are amazed at our son Eric's talent for making friends wherever he goes. He is a people magnet. No matter where he is, if there are kids around, he will have a playmate within minutes. He even befriends the adults.

Last summer we rented a house in the mountains of Colorado for a week. Within the first few hours, Eric had met most of the kids who lived on the street. All week he played basketball and rode bikes with his new friends. He made such an impression on one family that they stopped by before we left to get our name and address so they could visit Eric when they passed through Las Vegas on a trip they had planned.

When we went on a cruise last December, Eric made a new friend, Cody, before we even boarded the ship. They played together during that week on the ship, and still phone each other long distance. Eric is at their ranch in Utah now enjoying horses, jet skis, campfires, baseball, and swinging from ropes with his friend into their pond.

I took him to help me clean up a yard of a rental house my husband owns and within ten minutes their was another boy back there with him.

I watch him to analyze his gift, and have come to the conclusion that he loves people. He is always open to new relationships and I feel the main reason for his success in attracting people is he has no agenda except to have fun.

What if we approach every person we met with that attitude? If we really had an interest in that person and how we could make them smile? It would take the pressure off of us, because we would be focusing on them instead of ourselves. It would open doors and add more friendships as well as business relationships to our life.

You can get everything in life you want if you will just help enough other people get what they want.

Zig Ziglar

Chapter Five

Objections

What are objections? I believe over 95% of what people perceive as objections aren't objections at all. They are merely questions. If we really listen to people with a neutral attitude, meaning we don't care one way or the other what the outcome is, we will recognize people's responses as questions instead of objections.

How many times has a prospect said to you, "I object to your company! I object to your products! I object to your prices?" I have never personally experienced anything close to these comments.

Usually you will hear, "I don't have the time. I don't have the money. I can't sell. Is this one of those pyramid schemes?" Are these objections, or questions in disguise?

If you do a great job asking questions of your prospect and you listen to their responses, you'll realize that these comments are opportunities for you to show them how they can do this business. Once you have done that, it is up to them to decide how badly they want to change their life.

Remember, you are looking for people who are ready NOW to change their life and put your opportunity to work for them. If you show them how this is possible and they choose not to act, move on. Next. Check back with them in a month or two if they seem worth it.

When you hear these "classic objections," think of them as questions.
"Where would I find the time?"
"How can I get the money?"
"Do I have to sell?"
"Is this a legal business where I can really make money?"

Now you can answer their questions. You can show them how easy it is to use tools to leverage their time, so they can fit this business in with their everyday activities. Be creative and help them identify ways to get the money to start their business. Show them that this is a business where they give out information in order to find business partners. Establish the legitimacy of your company and this industry, explaining how they are compensated for their efforts.

I would love to put all my prospects up against my children. They wouldn't stand a chance. Objection doesn't even exist in my kids' minds. If they ask for something and I say no, they don't even blink an eye. They will continue asking.

"No" doesn't mean "no" to them. It means they need to rephrase the question, change the tone of voice, or just badger me to death! They honestly think they will get their request as long as they don't give up. On one hand I admire them for their tenacity, on the other hand I want to ring their necks for not listening to me in the first place and accepting my answer.

One time, Eric asked me if I would take him somewhere. I said no. So he instantly asked if he could ask Dad. I told him I couldn't believe he would even think to ask because there was a 99.9% chance of no. With a big smile on his face he ran upstairs to where his dad was. I yelled up to him, "What are you doing? I told you there was a 99.9% chance of no." Never missing a step he said, "I know, that means he might say yes!"

I had to laugh at how I opened the door for that one. It taught me to be more direct. More importantly it taught me to keep my mind open for the answer I want. When someone tells me no, that means no at this moment. If I apply Eric's philosophy, I will still be positive that sometime in the future, this person will be with me.

The most important point about this type of attitude is when I talk to the next person, my posture and belief are still strong. I'm not down because I heard a "no." I am positive and enthusiastic, excited to share my gift, looking for those that feel they deserve to open it.

Objections are opportunities. Opportunities for you to share information about this industry, your company, your products, your compensation plan, and how all of the above can impact someone's life. Have the tenacity of a child, knowing that to get what you want, you have to ask for it! Listen to what your prospect says, respond accordingly, and then collect a decision.

As a parent I get annoyed when my children ask me the same thing over and over again. But if I take their habit, and instead of asking one person over and over, ask many people once (with follow up if needed), I will find those few who are ready to join me on a wonderful journey. Then I will help them find a few. And you know the rest of the story. The numbers take over and before you know it, you have a thriving business.

For me, words are a form of action,
capable of influencing change.
                                    Ingrid Bengis

Chapter Six

Communication

Communication is a skill necessary for healthy, thriving relationships. How you communicate with others will determine your success in this business. It all starts with how you communicate with yourself.

Do you think of yourself as a winner? Do you tell yourself that you can do what you put your mind to, or do you automatically think you are going to fail? Your inward communication is expressed outwardly to others.

People want to be associated with winners. They are looking for a leader. It is hard for you to project that image if you feed your mind negative thoughts such as, "I'm not good enough. I don't deserve to succeed. Why would anyone want to be on my team?" If you think you are a loser, you'll act like a loser, people will see you as a loser and the only people you'll attract will be losers.

On the other hand, if you tell yourself you are successful, love this business, love people, love life, and have unlimited energy, then you will attract positive, enthusiastic, successful people to you.

I have seen this work time and again in our family. If my husband or I are in a bad mood and are short-tempered with our kids, raising our voices, the kids immediately adopt our attitude and mirror our actions. Pretty soon we have a houseful of grumpy people. The noise level goes up. Respect for each other goes down. It is all about attitude and once we change ours, the rest fall in line.

One of the most important means to achieve good communication is to listen. When you are engaged in conversation, the deepest respect you can pay the other person is to listen to what they are saying without interrupting them. So often we are either speaking or preparing to speak instead of listening to the person.

This is something I struggle with daily with my kids. It is so important to me that they know I am the parent, and they should listen to me. But when they say, "But mom, please listen to what I was going to tell you," I cut them short because I already know what they were going to tell me. I've heard it a million times before and I don't have the time to listen to the same argument at that moment! So I have an angry child who will probably get into trouble for talking back to me. Then I'm upset because there was an argument. It is a lose/lose situation.

How many times have you given a presentation where you talked a mile a minute and the prospect couldn't get a word in edge wise? You were so excited about what you had to say and you didn't want to forget anything, so you were afraid to stop talking!

What happens is the prospect may have some questions or comments along the way, but you will never hear them because you think it is more important for them to listen to your information. You feel that if they are listening to what you have to say all their questions will be answered anyway.

What really transpires is they get bored about halfway through your sales pitch. That is what they hear, a sales pitch. They put their guard up. And you are going to have a tough time connecting with them.

With my kids I try to catch myself and take the extra time to say, "OK, I will listen to what you have to say." By taking an extra minute and letting them speak, I can still impose the same decision on them, but at least they got some input on the situation and will respect me for caring enough to listen. It is probably the hardest habit to get into. And it is really just good manners!

The same goes with prospects. I make it a point to ask as many questions as I can and to have them do the talking. They feel that I value them and they are going to be more responsive to what I have to say when it's my turn to talk.

Listen to understand before speaking to be understood. If you make it a point to listen to what people are saying, you will connect with them. Instead of you pushing your opinions and reasons for doing this business on them, you can use their opinions and reasons to show them why this business is going to allow them to get what they want. You come across as caring for them instead of trying to get yourself ahead at their expense. And people want to think they are making their own decisions, not being "sold."

Communicate in their terms. It increases your credibility when you use the same context as they do. It's all about presenting your ideas in a way that the other person understands.

Remember, communication is much more than the words we say. Studies show that 10% of communication is through our words, 30% is by sound: inflections and noise level, and 60% is through our body language.

You could give the same presentation, word for word, but in one you are talking in a low monotone voice, slouched over. The other you have an animated voice, high energy, you're sitting up straight, leaning forward. You will communicate a totally different message in each even though you used the exact words.

When I talk to my children, the tone and volume of my voice makes a huge difference in how they respond. We all respond better to someone who we perceive as happy versus someone who is barking and angry.

When my children talk to me it is interesting how they use nonverbal communication. If they are trying to get something from me, they talk in a sweet voice, giving me special warm looks, moving towards me. If they aren't happy with me, they raise their voice, have a scowl on their face and back away from me.

We learn at a young age how to communicate. Most of how we communicate is done unconsciously. If you make the effort to be aware of how you use nonverbal as well as verbal communication, you will be better able to control the outcomes of your conversations.

For instance, Jenna, is brilliant at using communication to get what she wants. She approaches me with a sweet smile and pleasantly says, "*Maybe* I can have a graham cracker." Because of the way she phrased her statement most people would immediately respond by asking her if she wants a graham cracker, which I do. She lights up and says sure, like "What a great idea you had, Mom!" She is only three years old and she manipulates us like an old pro!

We need to learn from her how to get our prospects to ask to join our business, instead of us asking them! The conversation could go something like this: As you wrap up your presentation you could say, "John, maybe if we start working together now, you can build your business over the next 6 months and have the money you need for the down payment on that new home your wife has her eye on. Wouldn't she be surprised if you could purchase it a year ahead of your plan?"

John might reply, "If I sign up with this package, will I be able to leverage myself and make the most amount of money?" You then answer the question, get his credit card and welcome your new partner in business.

You have to work on yourself to become a better communicator. Listen to tapes, read books, and observe people. Be aware of your nonverbal as well as your verbal ways of communicating. Watch people's responses to what you say. Not so much their words, as their facial expressions and body language. It will tell you a lot about your communication skills.

And finally, practice, practice, practice. It will improve your confidence, improve your skills, and improve your results in your business and your personal relationships.

Never help a child with a task at
which he feels he can succeed.
                    Maria Montessori

Chapter Seven

My First Born

I remember when Kailee was born almost 16 years
ago. I was awestruck by the miracle of her and that
she belonged to me. I stared at her for hours. As she
grew, I fell deeper and deeper in love with her.

Remember the first distributor you signed up in
your organization, your first born? Did you stare at
the application? Were you exhilarated with the gift
of a new associate? Did you imagine all the big
plans you had for your newby?

I was excited to give all of my attention to Kailee,
treasuring each moment with her. When I was
pregnant with my second child, I was apprehensive
and fearful that I would not love him as much as I
loved her. I realize now how foolish and unrealistic
that fear was. (Aren't most fears?) I was just as
amazed and entranced by Eric, as I was Kailee.

So did you have an obsession with the first person you signed up? Were you fearful that if you signed more people to your team you would not have the time and energy to devote to them because you had too much emotion invested in your first born? It would be too hard to tear yourself away and "desert" them?

What I found with my children and my downline was that by dividing my time, I promoted independence. As your children grow (both in your business and in your family) you nurture and support them, while letting loose of the umbilical cord until you finally sever it when they are ready to be on their own.

It's a little scary for all involved, but the results and self-satisfaction everyone experiences will be very rewarding. You feel great accomplishment from teaching and developing someone to a point where they can be successful on their own. And your "child" will have the satisfaction of being self-reliant, knowing that they can become the "parent" and help others.

Everyone experiences growth, both on a personal and business level.

Life is a unique combination of "want to" and "how to," and we need to give equal attention to both.

Jim Rohn

Chapter Eight

"Training" Your Downline

You have just enrolled your superstar. This person is going to tear it up. You are so excited because this means a leg of your business is taken care of. You are on your way to major rank advancements.

We have all had a superstar – you know, the person who knows everyone, the person who has huge goals and dreams. You salivate just thinking of the paychecks to come.

You can't wait to get them trained so the money will start flowing your way. This is going to be a piece of cake. They are smart, personable, and they have what it takes. All you need to do is plug them into the system, supply them with the tools, do a couple of 3-way presentations and it will be a done deal.

You do a "get started" training, you take them to lunch to do a little dream building. You email them with all the training calls, meetings and events. They don't show up for anything. What are they waiting for? Why aren't they doing the business? What are they, stupid? You have called them everyday to show them you are there for them.

Have you ever potty trained a child? Let me tell you about potty training our daughter, Jenna. We knew she would be the easiest of the kids, the superstar. She was so smart and advanced for her age. And believe me, we as parents were very motivated. You see, if she wasn't potty trained, she couldn't go to preschool. So when she hadn't shown any interest yet at 2 ½, we figured we had 4 months to get her in gear.

We offered rewards. Nothing. I thought if I bought her the musical princess "Throne" that would do the trick. She loved walking by it and hearing the music, but there was no way she was going to sit on it! A friend gave her a potty training book that made obnoxious flushing noises. She loved it, but still preferred her diapers. We bought pretty princess panties, pull ups, told her she was a big girl, that she could go to school with her big brother if she went potty on the toilet, and once in awhile she would sit on the toilet, but she wouldn't perform. Sound like some of your distributors? There is a saying that comes to mind here: ---- or get off the pot!

There is nothing more frustrating than to know someone is capable and to see them do nothing. We were ready to pull our hair out with Jenna. The first day of school came. Jenna had been registered for over four months. I went to drop her brother off and told them that I wasn't having much luck potty training Jenna. She had a pull up on, but I knew their policy. The teacher said to leave her anyway and they would see what happened.

I came to pick the kids up and guess what- Jenna had gone potty on the toilet and had no accidents! From that day on she has been potty trained. Sure we have an accident once in awhile, but they are very rare.

I learned a great lesson. I couldn't control her mind and change her behavior. The timing had to be right for her. It had to be her idea and fit into her plan. The more frustrated I got, the less cooperative she was. Once I backed off and just accepted what will be will be, it happened when it was supposed to.

It's the same with your distributors. If and when they are ready, they will kick into gear. You just have to have patience and make sure to provide the training and support needed to be successful, *IF* they choose to be successful.

Once you let go of the feeling of responsibility for their performance, life becomes more pleasant and it frees up your time, energy and attitude to go after more prospects and to work with those distributors that deserve you time.

There are some things you don't have to know how it works. The main thing is that it works. While some people are studying the roots, others are picking the fruit. It just depends which end of this you want to get in on.

Jim Rohn

Chapter Nine

Duplication

Without duplication in your network marketing business you are like the rest of the dreamless, down trodden, miserable people- you have a job! In order to enjoy the benefits of residual income, you need to have duplication in your business. Leverage is what provides the ongoing checks while you are out enjoying the waves crashing on the beach, sipping on a tropical drink!

The first step is to find people who are motivated and teachable to duplicate your efforts. The second step is to teach them to plug into the system, and the third step is to push them out of the nest and let them fly. I think it is the third step of letting go that is the most difficult. You ask yourself a million questions. Are they ready to be on their own? Do they possess the necessary skills? What happens if they screw up? Maybe I should just do one more presentation for them. Have we all had these little conversations in our head before we send our downline out for their solo flight?

I thought I was comfortable with teaching people and sending them out on their own until our daughter, Kailee, got her learner's permit. You really want to face fear head on, put your whole family in the car and let your new teenage driver hit the freeway in Las Vegas through a construction zone! Did I mention I was 7 months pregnant? When she started randomly changing lanes in heavy traffic, cars honking, I thought I was going to have a heart attack. The good news is we all survived, with no accidents and Kailee got some great driving experience.

You may get the same queasy feeling when you turn your distributors lose to do their own presentations. Are they going to fumble through their first one, two, or three? Of course they are. You did. But they will never learn, if they don't start to do it for themselves. They need to experience the feeling, hear their own voice, listen to their prospects responses, and react to the different situations.

It's like Kailee learning to drive. I can't expect her to jump behind the steering wheel and drive perfectly just because she has over fifteen years of watching me drive. She has to experience it herself.

Sometimes we let our egos tell us that our people need us every step of the way. We want their success and ours too, therefore, we are afraid to take the risk of letting them fail a few times. But to really have true success, we absolutely need them to duplicate. So we need to set the example, train them well, and then step out of their way. Be by their side to pick them up and dust them off when necessary, but let them succeed or fail on their own.

Never believe that a few caring people can't change the world. For, indeed, that's all who ever have.

Margaret Mead

Chapter Ten

Teamwork

Last summer our son, Eric, and a couple of his friends set up a lemonade stand near our house. It was a prime location. There was plenty of traffic, a big tree to set up under for shade, and a corner for easy access. They were very proud of their venture.

This summer they got beaten to the punch by a nine year old who took their corner and set up a stand to sell apricots. After watching this kid peddle his goods for three days, my son and his friends decided to get in on the action and made plans to reclaim their corner.

They were up at 7:30 AM getting supplies and setting up their stand. My husband, Mark and I joked about the "Turf war" for the lemonade stand. Eric told us they were going to offer more value, wear uniforms to appear professional, and offer incentives for repeat business. Value, professionalism and repeat business are good lessons to be learned from an eleven year old!

At 9:30 AM I drove by to see how they were doing. The mother of the apricot salesman was there to help him set up shop. The "Turf War" had begun. The apricot salesman wanted to go down the street, obviously upset that the older boys moved in on his spot. His mom told him that he had customers coming back and they might not find him if he switched locations.

I suggested that he set up next to the older boys, let them sell the beverages and he could sell his apricots.

I pointed out that by working together, they would all do better. People who stopped for apricots might buy the beverages, and others who stopped for a drink might be interested in the apricots as well.

The older kids reluctantly agreed, telling him he could stay and sell his apricots. When I left, the apricot salesman was still having nothing to do with it and was trying to convince his mom to take him down the street. She was telling him this was a lesson in life, but he wasn't buying it.

Are you having "Turf Wars" in your mind? Do you have an abundance attitude or a scarcity attitude? Do you have a hard time helping others win, because you think it will mean you lose?

In network marketing, in raising a family, in practically every personal relationship you are involved in, helping others win increases your winning potential exponentially. There is no way around it. If you want success in your network marketing business, you must help others be successful.

You better learn to play team. Lone rangers may take off in their business, but they hit a ceiling because they don't duplicate. Without duplication, you have yourself a J.O.B.

To be a team player the first thing you need to do is let go of your ego. Listen to understand before being understood. You will attract people that care about your success as well as their own.

It has been amazing to see people who have done nothing to help themselves in their business come alive to help us reach a rank advancement. Some people have a stronger desire to feel needed and help others. The good news in network marketing is that they do end up helping themselves by helping others!

Look for people to join your team that are different than you. If you want to attract more people to your business, you need diverse personalities in your business. We all have different strengths, and when we come together as a team, we cover all bases and each can grow from the others knowledge.

Create a fun, enthusiastic and productive environment. People want to have fun and they want to be on a winning team. In our family, if there is one person whining and complaining, before you know it, the rest of us are grumpy. There is yelling, crying, picking on each other, and negative, unproductive energy fills our home. Make sure you nip negative, unproductive habits in the bud. Otherwise it will bring other team members down, and you will attract negative, unproductive people to your business.

Create a picture in your head of what you want your team to look like. What type of people do you want to work with? When you have a clear description of your perfect team player, then you need to become that type of person. Work on your own personal development and it will shape the team you attract.

There have been countless times in our family when we have had a difficult time with one of our kid's behavior. They will act out in a certain manner and we have no idea what caused it or how to change it. We try every form of punishment and discipline and still the bad behavior continues, and sometimes escalates.
We have found that if we stop focusing on their behavior, and focus on ours, 9 times out of 10 the problem resolves itself without the stress. We get the environment we were striving for. So when things aren't going the way you wish, take a look in the mirror. Focus on your behavior. Make sure you have a positive attitude, high energy, and a fun atmosphere surrounding you. You and your team will prosper.

Leadership and learning are indispensable to each other.

> *John F. Kennedy*

Chapter Eleven

Leadership

How do you become a leader? Simple. You find a follower.

Enroll a person in your network marketing business. Get married, have children. Could it be that easy? No, but it's a start. It is a fact that you need followers if you want to be a leader. But more importantly, you need a place to lead them to.

Great leaders know where they are going. They have a vision, a focus, a goal. They put a plan in motion to reach their destination. People join and follow them because they see the benefit of where they are heading and how they are getting there.

As a leader, you need to communicate your purpose to others in a compelling way. You must be crystal clear in your own mind about your goals, and make it appealing for others to follow. People have to see how their dreams can be achieved by partnering with you.

Success in network marketing comes from differentiating leading from managing. A leader identifies the goal, shows the plan to reach the destination, then leads by example and takes action.

Don't think people will "Do as I say, not as I do." It doesn't work with kids and it won't work with your downline either. Actions always speak louder than words. A great example of this opened my eyes recently to what an impact our actions make.

Our son, Tyler, was in our office one night and Mark was joking around with him. He asked him how old he was.

"My God, Dad, you know I'm five years old!"

I looked up, surprised, and asked him where he heard that saying. "Eric says it." Mark told him to say "my gosh" instead.

A few days later we were in the kitchen and our daughter spilled her drink. Out of my mouth pops,

"My God, Jenna! You need to be more careful."

It hit me immediately that I was the one that set the example for my kids. They are sponges, absorbing what we do and say. Then they put it to use, surprisingly in a correct context, at a later date.

The same is true with people on your team. If you are preaching to them about talking to people, giving presentations and sponsoring, you better be practicing it yourself. Your people will follow your lead. If you are spending more time managing, getting ready to get ready, then your people will be unproductive too.

A manager focuses on control. He or she is too busy fighting the battle instead of winning the war. What happens when you micro manage everyone and everything is you never step into productive mode. Don't look for perfection. Look for results.

Learn how to manage your time and teach your team time management skills. The biggest lesson in time management is learning how to say no. You might have to miss that Thursday night TV show, an afternoon shopping with a friend, your favorite sporting event, but it won't be a big sacrifice if you have a big WHY for your business. By possessing a huge "why" to keep you focused on your business, you will be able to say NO to distractions.

My kids know that as soon as they get home from school, they do their homework. After they are finished, then they can play with their friends. Sometimes they get no playtime because they have soccer practice. Once in awhile Eric will ask if he can do his homework later, but he always gets a no.

It has become a habit for them to start their homework immediately after school. The reward for them has been fantastic grades. They can see that when they apply themselves, they do well. They might miss out on a few hours of playtime, but they gain that and more in the long run, because they don't have to do make up work like some of their friends who watch too much TV and play after school.

By spending your time in a productive manner now, you will give yourself the luxury of spending your time any way you want in the future. And by setting the example for your team, you present the message that you are too busy to waste time and they will tend to waste less time as well.

To be a leader people look up to, you must take the ultimate responsibility for failure as well as success. You are going to experience both in your network marketing career. People respect someone who when faced with a struggle, focuses on the solution rather than looking to place blame. Pointing the finger is a waste of time and energy. While others look for a fall guy, spend your time productively. Solve the problem and move on.

In other words, avoid being in a political mode. Also stay away from management mode. Try to spend most of your time in productive mode. You will know you are there, because you will experience results.

I try to practice this philosophy with my family as well as my business. When I have kids arguing with each other and I confront the situation, nine times out of ten, I will hear, "He told me to shut up." "She was bossing me around."

I learned long ago to nip it in the bud and say, "I don't care who said what. You will get along starting immediately, or pay the consequences."

I have tried to be diplomatic and usually it just gets them more infuriated, the argument gets more intense and nothing but hurt feelings all around comes from it. My rule is to go immediately to the solution, learn from the experience, and pass on your knowledge.

When dealing with problems that arise in your business, it is best to handle them quickly and efficiently. People tend to focus on negativity and get their feathers ruffled. Why do you think Jerry Springer and Jenny Jones are still on TV? Give people positive things to talk about. Don't let others drag you down with them. When you deal with situations professionally, only speaking positively, you will earn the respect from your team.

A great leader always recognizes achievements of their team. People love seeing their name in print and hearing accolades about their accomplishments. It reinforces their commitment, and it will breed loyalty to you.

Mark and I have noticed a real difference with our kids when we focus on the positive things they do instead of harping on what they don't do. It is a hard discipline to get into, as we always want to correct the wrong behavior. We always expect the correct behavior without always acknowledging the correct behavior.

The best leaders possess a strong integrity, operate with honesty, and treat others by the "golden rule." They have respect for everyone they come in contact with and are always looking for the win-win opportunities.

Leaders succeed in life by helping others succeed, never at the expense of others.

Leaders surround themselves with a great team. There is synergy in numbers and where we are weak, others are strong.

Leaders are always growing. They work hard on personal development, reading, listening to audios, watching videos, working with coaches and attending seminars. In network marketing your business will grow in direct proportion to how much you grow.

As I am writing this section, I realize that the characteristics of a leader are characteristics I want my children to possess. I feel that on our path to become a great leader, we raise great leaders. Like the song from the "Lion King," it's *The Circle of Life.*

When you become a leader in network marketing, you are doubly rewarded with financial success as well as personal growth. The personal growth is even more valuable than the financial success.

When you talk to those who have become millionaires in network marketing, they will tell you that they would not trade the hard work, disappointments, struggles and challenges they faced on their journey for instant success, because they would not be the person they have become without the journey.

If someone took their money away, they could make it all over again because of the lessons they have learned. Having that confidence in yourself, knowing you can face anything life has to offer, is a great place to be.

Gratitude is not only the greatest of virtues, but the parent of all others.

Cicero

Chapter Twelve

Gratitude

Everyday we should start out with a thankful heart and mind. As the saying goes, make sure you "count your blessings" daily. When you appreciate what you have and express gratitude, more blessings flow your way. You open your mind to positive thoughts and occurrences and your glass is always half full instead of half empty. A positive attitude overcomes even the most difficult circumstances. Remember, it isn't what happens to you, it is what you do about it that counts.

Sometimes things happen in your life that at first send you for a loop, but upon deeper thought turn out to be an amazing gift. As I am writing this, I am eight months pregnant with our son, Max. He has been the light that has opened my heart to deep gratitude.

We have four beautiful children, a thriving network marketing business, and a great balance in our family. We thought everything was perfect just the way it was and had no intentions of any more children. So when I realized I was pregnant with number five, my first reaction was not one of complete excitement.

We have already talked about how we humans resist change and I couldn't imagine my life different, because it was so good as it was.

As my husband, Mark and I looked at the pregnancy test strip with its two pink lines, I started to cry. Mark wrapped his arms around me, and said, "This child could do amazing things. He could be President of the United States. Our children deserve to have another brother or sister to love." We started looking at all the positive ways this child was going to impact our family's lives, and turned our fears of change and responsibility into feelings of gratitude.

I am so thankful that God blessed us with Max. He trusts us to be great parents and is giving us another child to love and to raise, to bring more joy to the world. We are thrilled with the knowledge that we will have a big family and look forward to the years to come with the holiday gatherings and the laughter they will bring.

I told Mark we need to crank up this business because I want a big home in a great setting so all the kids will want to visit us often. I can visualize Christmas with everyone in the kitchen cooking and laughing, spending the night, with kids overflowing onto floors in sleeping bags and Grandpa Mark dressed up as Santa. I can see it, hear, it, taste, it, smell it and best of all feel it. What a wonderful, warm, happy feeling!

As I think about what I am grateful for I have to start with God and the way he has blessed my life with so much.

My husband, with his overwhelming energy and love for life, keeps everyday exciting and something to look forward to. I appreciate his unwavering love for his family and the dedication and balance he shares with us.

Our children, Kailee, Eric, Tyler, Jenna and Max have given me the most wonderful pair of glasses to view the world. I learn something new from all of them everyday and they have brought such joy and happiness to my life. They have helped me grow as a person, mother, wife and friend.

My parents have helped shape me into a happy, secure, loving adult by giving me unconditional love and support as a child. I am thankful to my husband's parents and sister for taking me into their family and giving me love and friendship.

For my dear friends with whom I have shared laughter and tears, good times and bad, through the years, I express gratitude for accepting me for who I am.

I am so grateful for my good health and like the relationships listed above, I do not take it for granted and commit everyday to giving it the attention it deserves.

I am thankful to the country I live in and the values and ideals it stands for. I appreciate the men and women who risk their lives to fight for our freedoms, and their families who pay the price as well.

I have so much gratitude to this industry, our company and the people who have had such a positive impact on our lives. From the founder and everyone at corporate, the speakers and the trainers, we have been made to feel special and we appreciate the friendships as well as the business support. From all the associates who have taken us under their wings and have become dear friends, we are amazed at the generosity sent our way.

I appreciate our upline, downline, and crossline and the friendships that have developed. It is exciting to share in the growth of each other. I am thankful for the teamwork that has come together and for the successes it has sprouted. I have been shown over and over again how much people care for each other.

As I reflect on all that I am thankful for, it lifts me emotionally and opens my spirit to infinite possibilities. We should all keep a gratitude list with us at all times, to pick us up when the going gets a little tough.

When you are grateful, your attitude does an about-face and you are able to open doors instead of slam them shut. When you are grateful, your positive attitude makes you happy, gives you enthusiasm, attracts others to you, which reinforces all of the above, poring unlimited blessings into your life.

You start to expect great things and open your mind to receive them. It is like a snowball effect. Once that ball is in motion, it keeps getting bigger and bigger and you create positive energy for more people. It is reciprocated back to you. This all starts with a little gratitude.

It is becoming good at the game of life. Problems always come up. When you experience gratitude, you create stronger, positive forces that balance against the negative forces giving you the power to overcome. Life will remain good. Therefore you will attract more good. When you apply this to your business, you encounter amazing results.

So express gratitude, and open yourself up to the abundant gifts life has to offer!

Many of life's failures are people who did not realize how close they were to success when they gave up.

Thomas Edison

Final Thoughts

Growing your network marketing business and raising a family are like wild roller coaster rides. As you wait in line for your turn, you stare at the monstrosity you are about to strap yourself into. You watch the people as they unload, looking at their faces to gage their reaction to the experience. Do you identify with the people who are green and holding their stomachs, or do you fixate on the people who come bouncing off, laughing and screaming that they want to get back in line for another ride?

When you start with a network marketing opportunity you might experience the same emotions as waiting in line for the roller coaster. It all sounds good and it could provide you with the ride of your life, but what about those big ups and downs? What fast curves and bumps will you encounter? Are you filled with fear that makes your stomach turn, or can you see past that to the adventure of greater opportunity?

My advice is to commit to the excitement and the fun. Tell yourself you will be one of the people hopping off at the ride's end, racing to get back in line. It is all right to experience fear, it keeps your senses alert, but you must control it and channel it so you live life to your full potential. Don't let fear control you and stop you from enjoying all the wonderful treasures life has to offer. When you get to the front of the line, make the commitment and strap yourself in for the ride.

You inevitably start out by slowly climbing, inch by inch, up the big hill. You have feelings of anticipation, knowing that once you get to the top, you will come racing down into the unknown. There's that split second at the top, where you are just hanging in limbo, not having started your descent. It seems like an eternity, as a million thoughts race through your mind.

"What am I doing here? Am I ready to go down? Am I holding on tight enough? Should I keep my eyes closed or open? I'm going to kill the person who talked me into this! I'm going to thank the person who talked me into this. This is so exciting! I can't wait to feel the wind racing past me as we go down. I wonder if there is a hairpin turn or a corkscrew at the bottom of this hill? Wait till I tell my friends what I did!"

You plummet down the hill, hit the turns, encounter more hills and valleys and finally come pulling in at the end and disembark. Whether you think it was the greatest experience in your life, or think you wouldn't be caught dead on another roller coaster, you will at least feel the satisfaction of saying, "I did it."

As you ride the network marketing roller coaster, you will experience the excitement, fear, exhilaration, stomach aches, thrills, accomplishment and love. How does love fit in? As you go up and down the hills, face the challenges, break through and enjoy the rewards, you feel love for yourself, for the person you have become. As you hit the turns and corkscrews and realize that there are always people who care for you and who you care for around those corners, you experience love for others and that love is reciprocated.

Just like the roller coaster, raising a family has its ups and downs. It has been the most rewarding experience in my life. I wouldn't trade it for anything. I can't think of one thing that has given me more happiness, pride and laughter.

There are days when it is frustrating, painful and frankly quite scary. Kids don't come with directions. You learn as you go.

Fortunately, in network marketing you learn from those that have gone ahead of you. There is a built in support system to plug into and you have a team that has a vested interest in helping you succeed.

It's up to you to get on the ride. Don't sit on the sidelines watching others take your turn. Don't let your fears stop you from living huge. You deserve to grab your dreams. You were put on this earth to have it all and to give it your all. Network marketing can provide you with the means to live an abundant rewarding life if you just jump on board.

The number one thing to remember for your success in network marketing is, **do not quit!** This is a business that takes time to develop. Unlike studying to be a doctor or a lawyer, after you have put over a decade into preparing for your career, you aren't left with hundreds of thousands of dollars of school loans, hoping to start out with that six figure income. You are not looking forward to 50 plus hours a week at the J.O.B.

In network marketing while you "study" to be an entrepreneur, you make money along the way. You can pay off debt, not accumulate student loans. You enjoy the travel, time with your family and friends, your hobbies, instead of grinding away at a J.O.B. And the best part is that money you are making keeps showing up in your mailbox over and over again, no matter what you are doing!

During the future doctor's journey were there difficult times where he or she wanted to quit? You bet. During your journey in your home -based business will there be times that you want to jump ship? Of course. But don't do it. It's when the going gets tough, that personal as well as financial growth will break through. If you stick with it, you will reap the rewards. And they are so worth it. The quality of the life you lead when you have complete time and financial freedom is well worth a few years of commitment.

When you become a parent, you are not thinking, "I'll give this a try for six months to a year and see how I like it." You better know up front that you are in it for the long haul. There will be plenty of times that you want to throw your hands up in the air and say, "I've had it! I can't take any more!"

But then the next moment, those children of yours will give you a look, a hug, or say just the right thing to catch you off guard and warm your heart to them, making you forget why you were ready to blow a gasket just a few minutes before.

Your network marketing business is your child. Make a commitment to yourself to have it all. Give yourself the time to "raise your child" into the adulthood of a thriving, exciting business.

From being pregnant to having a daughter that is turning sixteen, I can see first hand what the beginning is like and what years of love, commitment and attention produce. I'm in the toddler stage of my network marketing career, but I can see what the teenage stage will bring me and I can't wait! I have met others who have reached their goals and are living their dreams and they all say it was worth the times where they had fear and doubts.

Mark and I enjoy the financial rewards from our business and are excited because it just keeps growing. Every week our checks get bigger and bigger. More importantly, we can't believe the lifestyle we have and are able to share with others. We make choices that most people can't. We appreciate the time we have, to do what we want with who we want. Our kids have an unbelievable balance in their lives with both parents at home. They see us work together and they are a part of our business, helping us with tasks and traveling with us to company activities.

We are living our dream and everyday we look forward to new people, experiences and good fortune. We are contributing to those around us, and teaching good values to our children.

Live your dream. Dedicate your life to getting what you deserve by helping others get what they deserve. Take control of your life and make choices that propel you in the direction you desire instead of waiting for life to happen to you.

Embrace your business with enthusiasm and a commitment for success and you will be rewarded with a gift of an unbelievable life for you and your loved ones.